Happy Birthday!

A Book About Birthdays, Dreams And Wishes

By Penelope Dyan

Bellissima Publishing, LLC
Jamul, California
www.bellissimapublishing.com

copyright © 2009 by Penny D. Weigand

All rights reserved. No part of this book may be
reproduced or transmitted in any form or by any means,
electronic or mechanical, including photocopying,
recording, or by any other means, or by any information or
storage retrieval system, without permission from the publisher.

ISBN 1-935118-73-0
First Edition

For all you birthday girls and boys,
Because birthdays are more than presents and toys!

Happy Birthday!
Bellissima Publishing, LLC

Introduction

Birthdays are about more than just cakes, balloons and presents, although those are fun. A birthday means you are one year older; and with each year you will be accomplishing new things, and have new dreams, and you will be growing into adulthood. Children can't wait to become adults and to have all their dreams come true; and they need to be encouraged to follow their dreams, because dreams really can come true if you believe in yourself and your dreams.

Penelope Dyan encourages her young readers to hold steadfast to their dreams, and her message for parents is that they can make their dreams come true as well, because dreams have no limit; and anything is possible, and people can make their dreams come true!

Dyan is the author of award winning 'Surfer Girl,' the first book in the Surfer Girl Book Series. Surfer Girl was the winner of best teen book at the 2008 New York Book Festival and best teen book at the 2008 Hollywood book Festival and is recognized by Girls Voices In Literature Database, Miami University Florida. Surfer girl is also ranked fifth on the Australian Pukeke top ten reading list for early teen girls, and her book "A Book For Girls About Being A Girl" is ranked third in poetry for girls ages 5-9. Dyan is also a former teacher and an attorney, proving once again that you can't go wrong with a Bellissima Book.

Give your favorite person this book for their birthday and watch them smile, because you just can't go wrong with a dream or a Bellissima Book

Happy Birthday!
Bellissima Publishing, LLC

Happy Birthday!

A Book About Birthdays, Dreams And Wishes

By Penelope Dyan

Today is your birthday or (if not) will be soon,
So here for you is a great big balloon!

And here for you is a great big cake;
Don't eat it all at once, for goodness sake!

Mom says birthdays come but once a year,
And before you know it the next is here.

AND before you KNOW it I am told,
You are over the hill and VERY old!

When you are little you have lots of dreams,
Of growing up to be princesses or kings.
And here is something that I know,
When you are little growing up seems slow.

And when you are big like your mom or your dad,
Sometimes birthdays can make you sad.
Because it is a fact and so very true,
That there is still so much they want to do!
And for them time seems about gone,
Even though they are really wrong.

They say they want the clock to stop,
Before their bodies have to drop.

And then they say they will push up roses,
Under the ground, and ABOVE their noses!
And so they tell you to seize the day,
So that life will go YOUR way!

So here is my birthday advice for you;
Make sure that all your dreams come true!
And when you blow out the candles on your cake,
Remember the wishes that you make!
Because YOU can make your wishes come true,
Making dreams come true is up to YOU!

And please remember it is NEVER too late,
Until you're standing at heaven's gate!

So be a teacher, a cook, a mom or dad...

A fireman, farmer...

Singer...

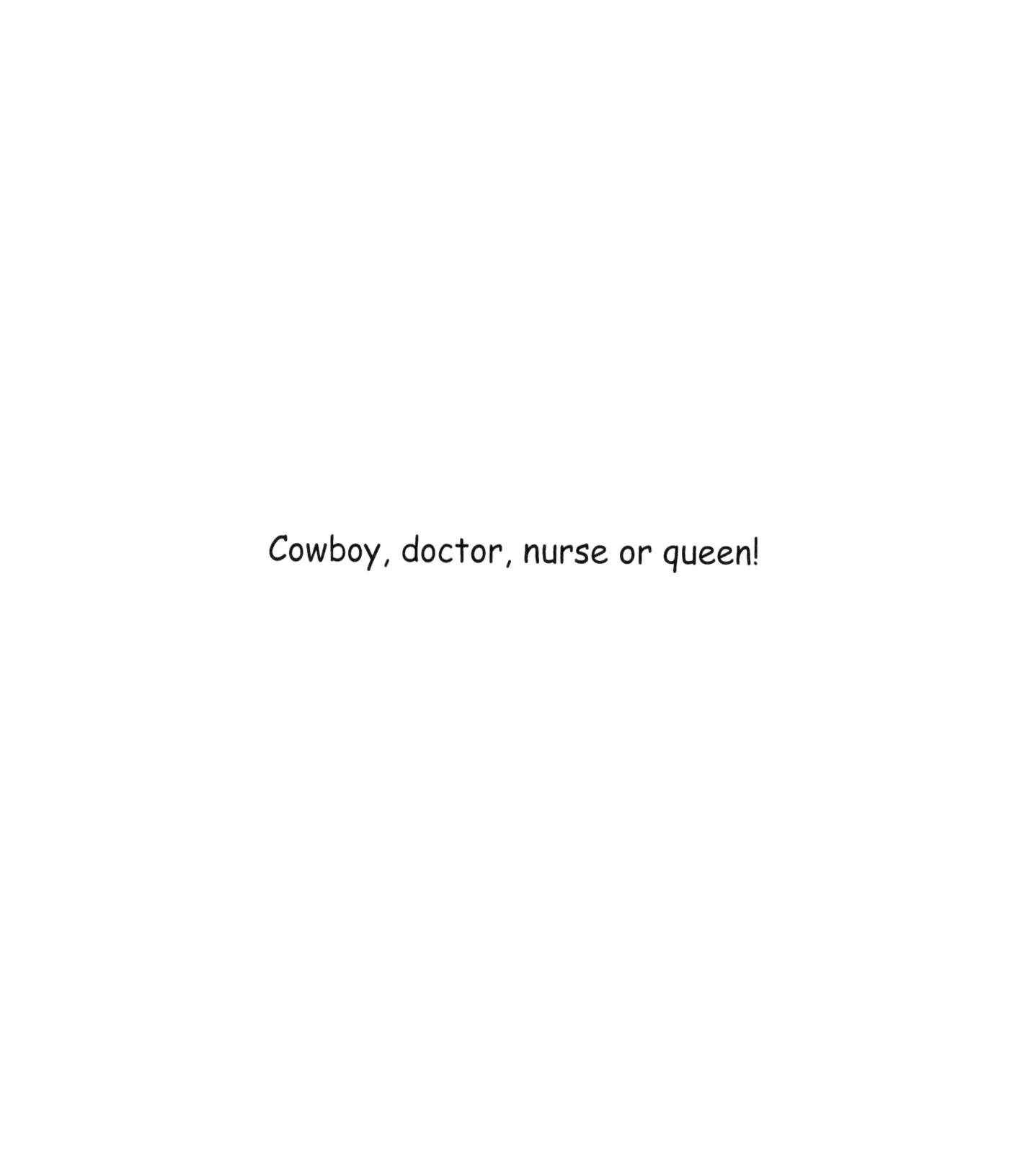

Cowboy, doctor, nurse or queen!

Just PLEASE remember to follow YOUR dream.
Because it is important, and very true,
That everyone deserves for their dreams to come true.
So HAPPY BIRTHDAY! HAPPY BIRTHDAY to you!
Have a VERY happy day, no matter WHAT you do!
And PLEASE pay attention, and follow my advice,
And YOUR life will be oh so nice!
Because happiness is NOT about gifts or money,
And dreams coming true will make your life sunny!

And then when you go to bed at night,
The universe will be balanced and EVERYTHING right!

The End
is not the end just because the party is over.

www.ingramcontent.com/pod-product-compliance
Ingram Content Group UK Ltd.
Pitfield, Milton Keynes, MK11 3LW, UK
UKHW060137240426
12048UKWH00002B/73